To the One Who Raped Me

Dustin Brookshire

Sibling Rivalry Press
Alexander, Arkansas
www.SiblingRivalryPress.com

To the One Who Raped Me

Copyright © 2012 by Dustin Brookshire.

Author photograph by Jeffrey Lofgreen. Used by permission.

Cover design by Mona Z. Kraculdy.

All rights reserved. No part of this book may be reproduced or republished without written consent from the publisher, except by reviewers who may quote brief excerpts in connection with a review in a newspaper, magazine, or electronic publication; nor may any part of this book be reproduced, stored in a retrieval system, or transmitted in any form, or by any means be recorded without written consent of the publisher.

Sibling Rivalry Press, LLC
13913 Magnolia Glen Drive
Alexander, AR 72002

www.siblingrivalrypress.com
info@siblingrivalrypress.com

ISBN: 978-1-937420-20-8

First Sibling Rivalry Press Edition, August 2012.

There are 525,600 minutes in a non-leap year. That makes 31,536,000 seconds in every year. So: 31,536,000 divided by 248,300 comes to one **SEXUAL ASSAULT** *every 127 seconds, or about one every two minutes.*

CONTENTS

I Don't Like to Say the Word Rape — 9

Soap — 10

Law & Order: SVU — 12

In the Movies — 13

Thief in the Night — 15

Wreckage — 16

How Can I Tell Them — 18

Vocal — 19

No Comedy in Tragedy — 21

My Therapist Asks What Image Haunts Me — 22

Living Vicariously Through *Extremities* — 24

A Poem for a New Lover — 25

The Flowerbed of Regret — 27

To the One Who Raped Me — 28

To the One Who Raped Me

FLASHBACKS are when **MEMORIES** of past **TRAUMAS** feel as if they are taking place in the current moment.

These memories can take many forms: dreams, sounds, smells, images, body sensations, or overwhelming emotions. This re-experience of the **TRAUMA** often seems to come from nowhere and therefore blurs the lines between past and present, leaving the individual feeling **ANXIOUS**, **SCARED**, **POWERLESS**, or any other emotions that they felt at the time of the **TRAUMA**.

I DON'T LIKE TO SAY THE WORD RAPE

When I say the word rape
I think of Jodie Foster in *The Accused*.
I envision Jodie on the stand
telling the jury she knew who was inside.
The defendant interrupting
to ask how she knew if her eyes were covered.
Jodie replies,
Because they were chanting his name.

But that isn't how it happened.
There was *No*.
Silence.
Him coming inside.

SOAP

The smell of Ivory burns my mind:
The shower after—
how I barely touched myself,
let the water wash over me.
I won't. No. I can't forget his smell.

Ivory, so close to irony,
how we once craved to be close,
bodies connected, but that night
he took what he wanted,
left me the smell of Ivory.

Males are the least likely to report a **SEXUAL ASSAULT**, *though they make up about 10% of all victims.*

LAW & ORDER: SVU

I do not watch for open endings.

I watch to see the rapist slammed
against the interrogation room wall,
to stand before the judge
and receive a hefty sentence.

I imagine what isn't:
The rapist victimized in prison.
His breakdown. A suicide attempt.
A life without redemption.

IN THE MOVIES

She rejects him with a laugh.

I cringe.

She strides to the bathroom. Doesn't notice
his eyes locked, fist pressed into the bar.

I cringe.

Her girl friend asks, *You'll catch a cab?*
He overhears, *Yes.*

I cringe.

He sees tequila shots keeping her company.
He licks the right upper corner of his lip.

I cringe.

He follows her out. She almost falls.
The taxi pulls up. His hand grips her elbow.

I whisper: *Run girl, run.*
You'll never be the same again.

Movies and TV shows that show **RAPE, SEXUAL ASSAULT, INCEST,** *and* **CHILD SEXUAL ABUSE** *can be very difficult for survivors to watch.*

Remember that you do not have to watch TV shows or movies. Watch because you want to watch, not because you feel like you **HAVE TO** *or because watching TV has become a habit!*

THIEF IN THE NIGHT

He didn't come like a thief
in the night; he came like a man
determined, obsessed,
who needed to mark his spoils—
like my childhood neighbor's Doberman.
Both on quests for territory.
They came to lay claim.

I could have ended up mauled—
mother sobbing, shaking,
hyperventilating,
cursing the Doberman.
Instead, with my air rifle,
a few BBs changed a growling dog
to a whelping mutt en route home.

There was no BB gun
when he came
inside me.
I could have screamed
like I was told to as a child
if someone touched me
inappropriately. Instead—
I asked him, politely, not to.
Then I told him no.
Then lay paralyzed,
hands pressed to the bed
like Jesus's hands to the cross.

WRECKAGE

After the wreck on 10th Street,
when the van smashed into my car,
I called him—too afraid to call my parents.
He drove me home. He helped me
to my bedroom as I limped.
He stayed the night, called four times
the next day. How was I to know
a week later he would wreck me?

There are many emotional and psychological reactions that victims of **RAPE** and **SEXUAL ASSAULT** can experience. One of the most common of these is **DEPRESSION**.

DEPRESSION is not a sign of weakness, and it is not something that someone can make him/herself "**SNAP** out of."

HOW CAN I TELL THEM

My mother,
after *those* news stories,
said *I'd kill anyone who hurt my boys.*
I believed her. I still believe.

My father
had me stand in front of a barbwire fence
to teach me not to fear a baseball,
to be a man's man.

VOCAL

I was raped
isn't like saying,
I need a glass of water.
Or, *May I go to the bathroom.*

It is flame to skin.

Knife stabbed in stomach,
then twisted.

But, the words open a cage door.
I will never go back in.

VICTIMS *of* **SEXUAL ASSAULT** *are:*

3 times more likely to suffer from depression.

6 times more likely to suffer from post-traumatic stress disorder.

13 times more likely to abuse alcohol.

26 times more likely to abuse drugs.

4 times more likely to contemplate suicide.

NO COMEDY IN TRAGEDY

Popcorn between my legs,
left arm rests on Paul's right,
we watch *The Hills Have Eyes 2*.
I twist. Heart races. Mouth goes dry
when the guy cuts her pants.
People laugh as he bends her over a table.
I turn to see their faces.

I tug on Paul's jacket,
They're laughing. They are fucking laughing.
He says, *Calm down.* I can't.
It's like they are laughing at me.

MY THERAPIST ASKS
WHAT IMAGE HAUNTS ME

In the bathroom
I push out his cum
like a mother who knows
her baby is stillborn.
When it is done, it isn't done.
The feeling of him still clings.

Approximately 2/3 of **RAPES** *are committed by someone known to the victim.*

LIVING VICARIOUSLY THROUGH EXTREMITIES

He never saw it coming.

The bug spray to his eyes.
The poker. The fireplace.
The embers of revenge in her eyes.
The loss of power through his hands
like water through a sieve.

A POEM FOR A NEW LOVER

I do not fear sex with a lover
who listens to my yes's,
obeys my no's.
I fear telling him—

fear the way my lover's touch
will change—
that he'll lose lust
and look with worry
once he knows.
That he'll see in me a victim,
not the person he needs to know.

Approximately 2/3 of **RAPES** *are committed by someone known to the victim. 28% are an* **INTIMATE**.

THE FLOWERBED OF REGRET

His hands flare like chrysanthemums
in the movies: wide to cover your mouth,
wide to press your hands
into the bed.
That night, it wasn't a movie,
when he pressed his hands into mine,
into the mattress I later burned.
His hands were once beautiful
like a bed of chrysanthemums
when they stroked my jaw line,
caressed my back, pulled me into him.
And, now, I still feel his hands
that are smaller than mine
as I wake from the repeating nightmare.
Goddammit, why didn't you fight?

TO THE ONE WHO RAPED ME

I cringe now when there's a rape scene
in a movie. My stomach cramps
like a bully has hit me.
I turn cold.
Beads of sweat form a crown
of shame across my forehead.

I want your mother to know—
to question where she went wrong.
I want you to stare into her eyes
as she asks you. Feel her pain.

I often think of ways you could die—
car wreck, allergic reaction, a robbery.
My therapist says it is normal
to have these thoughts, to want you
to die, but important to admit
your suffering won't bring me happiness.

What I want is impossible:
to erase the moment after,
when you looked at me and smiled.

ACKNOWLEDGEMENTS & NOTES

I would like to thank the editors of the following publications for publishing poems from this collection in earlier or current drafts:

"Wreckage" ~ *Ducts*

"Soap," "Vocal," & "The Flowerbed of Regret" ~ *Subtle Tea*

"Thief in the Night" ~ *Blue Fifth Review*

"In The Movies" ~ *Apparatus*

"I Don't Like To Say The Word Rape," "No Comedy in Tragedy," & "Living Vicariously Through *Extremities*" ~ *Shape of a Box*

All of the facts/statistics found throughout the chapbook are taken from the Rape, Abuse, & Incest National Network website: www.rainn.org

First line of "The Flowerbed of Regret" is from Christopher Tozier's "Summer Evening, Hopper 1947."

Chris, you listened when I couldn't tell anyone else; you read the poems when I couldn't show anyone else. Dr. Gup, you're the reason why I am able to say the word rape; you helped me see that I can still hold my head high. Beth, you changed the way I experience poetry. Shaindel, you changed the path. I'm indebted to you all—THANK YOU.

ABOUT THE POET

Dustin Brookshire is a poet and activist who resides in Atlanta, Georgia. Dustin's work has been honored by the Alabama State Poetry Society and Oregon Poetry Association and nominated for a Pushcart Prize. His poems have been published by *Ocho, Oranges & Sardines, Shape of Box, SubtleTea, Apparatus, Ouroboros, qarrtsiluni,* and other publications as well as the anthology *Divining Divas: 100 Gay Poets on Their Muses* (Lethe Press, 2012).

www.dustinbrookshire.com

ABOUT THE PUBLISHER

The mission of **Sibling Rivalry Press** is to develop, publish, and promote outlaw artistic talent—those projects which inspire people to read, challenge, and ponder the complexities of life in dark rooms, under blankets by cell-phone illumination, in the backseats of cars, and on spring-day park benches next to people reading Beth Gylys and Denise Duhamel.

We believe in literary rock stars.

www.siblingrivalrypress.com

CPSIA information can be obtained at www.ICGtesting.com
Printed in the USA
LVOW060127020712

288411LV00004B/3/P